Kids' Words
When a Parent has Cancer

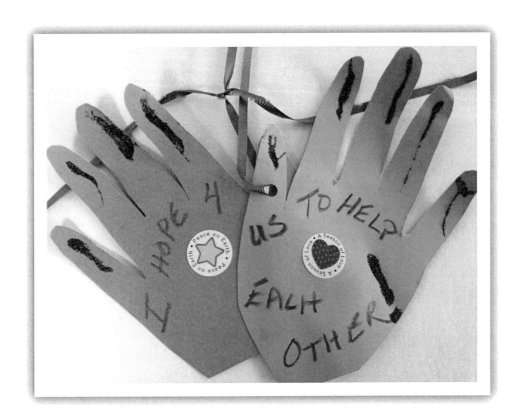

Written by Madelyn Case, Ph.D., Jeanne Curry, BN, CNS, and Lorraine Hart, Ph.D,
with quotes and artwork from the kids of Kids Alive! Support for Children of Parents with Cancer

Table of Contents

What the Kids Say About Kids Alive

Coming to Kids Alive gives you a group of people who understand you and are there to support you. Being a part of the group helps you talk about your story and how you and your family have been impacted. Kids Alive provides discussions to help you understand cancer and what it does. If you feel upset, angry or afraid, it gives you a safe place to express yourself. Even though your friends don't understand your situation, the friends you make here will, and you will be able to relate to one another through fun activities

Prologue

⚜

The occurrence of cancer in the family is traumatic for everyone, both in the family, and for loved ones outside the family. For children especially, there are changes which they have never before experienced: absences of the cancer patient, diminished attention to the child, patterns of behavior that are new and unfamiliar. Children cope in whatever ways they can, often appearing to other family members as inappropriate, immature, or self-centered. Children's real feelings are often not recognized.

The impetus behind forming *Kids Alive! Support for Children of Parents with Cancer* was to address this lack of awareness of the child's journey when his/her parent is diagnosed. A major purpose of Kids Alive is to help children and adolescents express their emotions. To do so, we have employed as many modalities as possible, including music, drama, art, role-playing and oral sharing. We experience, in story and play-acting, the Hero's Journey; that is, the experiencing of a traumatic event, feelings of depression and anxiety, discovery of allies (friends), overcoming many obstacles and changes, and realizing one's self as a hero, with qualities of strength, confidence, and compassion. An aspect of compassion is the need to help others, to inspire, and to give back.

With this in mind, members of Kids Alive determined to create a book which would support going through the experience of a parent being diagnosed with cancer. Knowing that sharing feelings helps others to identify their own feelings, kids recalled perceptions and behaviors from their personal journeys. The "Kids' Words" in this book are the comments from Kids Alive members and junior volunteers, in Spring, 2014. The art illustrations have been taken from art sessions that span the life of Kids Alive. These are all products of children and teens in Kids Alive. The authors added comments to parents, and suggestions for help.

Kids Alive is sponsored by:
Porter Adventist Hospital and Porter Hospital
Foundation

*We would like to express our gratitude to both
Porter Adventist Hospital and Porter Hospital
Foundation for their significant and consistent
support since the inception of Kids Alive in 1995.
—The Authors*

Chapter 1:
A Parent is Diagnosed with Cancer

The quotes in this chapter are what the kids said when asked...

What was it like when you found out your parent had cancer?

"I was scared my mom would die, but I was also angry that this could happen; I did not understand why this was happening to my mom...why not someone else?"

My mom was in bed, I was sad. —*Galilea, age 8*

"I got very scared that
my mom was not going to
get better."

"At first I did
not know what
would happen
because of the
cancer because
I had not
seen the effects
of cancer
treatment, but
it did scare
me."

"I was really confused and scared. I did not know what a tumor was and had a lot of questions. I was thankful that my parents were there to answer my questions."

Other thoughts...

"... do not like the limitations it put on our family to make plans."

"... nervous for what is coming."

"... disappointments and changed plans."

"... angry at the insurance company."

"... did not like people telling me they knew just how I was feeling."

"... anger that people were not taking this seriously."

What families should know

Cancer diagnoses often seem to appear out of the blue and may provoke intense anxiety in all family members. Parents are trying to deal with their own feelings as well as process all the choices that must be made. In the middle of this, they must decide when and what to tell their children while trying to protect them from the worst of the distress. Often because parents are dealing with their own feelings there is little time or emotional energy to support their children's feelings. Yet this is just as critical a time for kids as it is for the parents, and children will do better overall with help dealing with this stress and anxiety.

What to do

- Listen to your kid's feelings without judgment.

- Offer extra support such as a hug.

- Affirm that this is something the whole family is going through and you will be there with them.

- Share with your children what you know, not what you fear. Sharing the facts can be reassuring to children and will let them know you can be trusted.

Chapter 2:
Going Through Treatment

Treatment adds its own level of stress for everyone. Kids report that they really struggle watching their parent go through treatment. Here are some descriptions.

"I didn't really understand how serious the situation was at home, but as it got worse, I became more stressed at home, at school and with friends, which made my grades drop. I struggled to find people I could relate to."

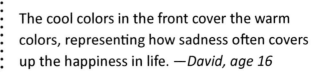

The cool colors in the front cover the warm colors, representing how sadness often covers up the happiness in life. —*David, age 16*

"It was hard to watch my dad so sick. He was always so strong and brave and when he was sick, he became strong and brave in a different way. It was hard to see him at the hospital and not feeling well. It was hard because my friends didn't understand. I often felt alone."

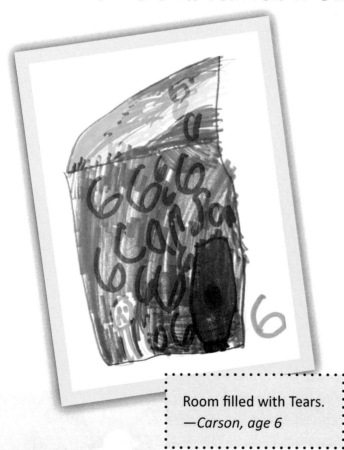

Room filled with Tears.
—*Carson, age 6*

"It was scary and I thought she was going to die. It was getting worse and I went home crying every night."

"I remember being angry with my mom because she was too sick and tired to take me places or hang out with me."

Before cancer and during cancer, "Ugh, Madi, can you take out the dog?" —*Madison, age 9*

"Missing the parent when they can only stay in bed."

Other thoughts...

"... family time stops."

"... people don't understand your battlo."

"... treatment makes parent even more sick before they get better."

"... good days and bad days—unpredictable ... big changes—not being able to see your parent."

What families should know

Treatment is a very stressful time for all of the family. In addition to taking up time and causing the patient to feel unwell, things are often very chaotic and events that would normally take place in family life tend to be disrupted and priorities shift drastically. Children's lives change in unexpected ways such as not being able to do their normal activities, feeling more responsible for the family, and in fact having more responsibilities around the house. In addition, most of family life now revolves around the patient, not the child, which can be a big change.

What to do

- Continue to be open about plans and encourage your kids to talk about feelings and/or questions they might have.

- Try to be sensitive to children's anxieties while being realistic about what is required to care for the patient.

- This is a good time to rely on help from family and friends to make sure your child's life is as consistent as possible.

Chapter 3:
How Did I Show People I Was Upset?

❋

During the Kids Alive group sessions, we express feelings in many different ways—through art, music, drawing, and skits. What we have come to appreciate is how often the families are not sure what the child is experiencing, and that kids often don't share. Here are some recollections of Kids Alive members.

"I stayed in my room a lot, frowning. I just got really emotional with my feelings. I was really nervous because what always pops into your mind is the worst thing possible. I showed that by wandering off in class or a conversation."

What it feels like when you find out your parent has cancer. —*Vaughan, age 6*

"I found myself to be weepy and weird at times."

"I talked about my feelings and sometimes cut myself off from interaction with people. I also wrote a lot of things down, both in journals and in poems or stories to try processing how I felt."

The dragon is cancer.
—*Gavin, age 9*

"I didn't show people I was upset because I didn't feel like everyone helping and stuff. I would end up going somewhere to decompress."

"I became very busy."

The dragon represents the depression of cancer, the last glimmer of happiness is in the tail. —*Addison, age 10*

"At times I would be mad at nothing and then people figured out that I just didn't know what to do."

Other thoughts...

We experienced all of these things!

lack of focus

anger

wanting to be alone

bottled up sadness

poor behavior

withdrawal from others

insomnia

What families should know

Both adults and children are going to be upset during the cancer journey. Frightened, angry, lonely or uncertain feelings are common and may be expressed in very individualized ways. Although some children can tell you what they're feeling, they also may act out feelings in unexpected ways. It is important to understand that sometimes your child's surprising behavior is a way of expressing frustration, anger or sadness. In addition, children will try to protect you by hiding feelings. It is OK to ask them what is going on.

What to do

- Recognize the behavior in your child that indicates s/he is struggling.

- Check out their feelings; don't assume you know what they are.

- Realize that your child may not be comfortable discussing their feelings with you. Since children often want to protect their parents, suggest another adult with whom the child can discuss their feelings if they so desire. Examples might be other family members, teachers, or friends of the family.

Chapter 4:
What Would I Do Differently

One of the outcomes of this journey is learning about yourself and gaining tools to cope with whatever life may bring. Although we don't always verbalize this in group, when we asked the question, the kids had many answers!

"I think I learned that showing my emotions is not a bad thing. It can really help if you show your emotions."

"I learned to spend more time with friends and family".

What I would do differently:

"I would not be so loud and (I would) spend time with my grandfather (my mom or my dad) while I could."

"I would go back and not argue with her as much."

"Not listen to people who judge you or your family."

Other thoughts...

"... don't argue
so much."

"... don't be afraid
to ask for help."

"... don't be afraid
to receive help."

"...don't feel you
need to be strong."

perspective
is key

What families should know

In looking back over the experience, most people, including kids, can tell you what they learned about themselves and what they would do differently. It is more than ok to have this discussion with your children. Since neither children nor adults like being put on the spot, you might find it most helpful for the entire family to talk about those insights.

 # What to do

- Make time as a family to discuss the things you have learned about yourself while on the cancer journey.

- Be open with your children about what things you wish you had done differently. Let the kids know this is a healthy part of coping with cancer.

- Accept their preference to talk about it or not.

Chapter 5:
What I Wish Someone Had Done Differently

We wanted to pass on some things families tried that didn't work so well. We know all of the families acted with the best of intentions, but the kids were clear about what they wished had happened.

"Be honest—being open about what is going on. Sometimes protection is scarier than the truth."

"I wish someone had told me about Kids Alive."

—*Clayton, age 13*

"I wish my family would understand my anxiety problems. I wish people didn't think depression just went away."

How precious time is.
—*Meghan, age 24*

"I wish we could have gone to the doctor earlier. I also wish I would have started online school sooner, it has helped immensely."

The one place that is happy other than home- Kids Alive.
—*Rylee, age 12*

"People need to feel loved."

"People need to be more observant and ask how 'YOU' are doing"

Other thoughts...

"... when people offer help, accept it."

"... think before you speak (i.e., jokes about cancer.)"

"... know it is ok to cry."

"... wish people would understand what's going on and were more observant."

What families should know

Families are sometimes tempted to protect their children by not being honest. When a crisis occurs, parents worry that their children will be traumatized or emotionally scarred, and as a result sometimes avoid revealing the true nature of the crisis to their children. But children know that a major change has occurred. Their imaginations create stories which may be much scarier than the truth, and children may be feeling very angry, feeling that they have not been told the whole story. But, since they want to be good children, they do not reveal their fears and anxieties in order to protect their parents. In addition to the truthfulness, children most want understanding.

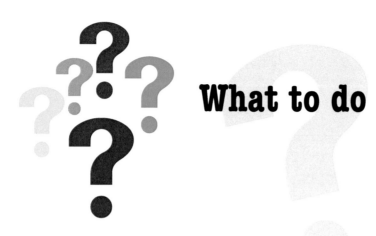

What to do

- Tell your children what you know, not what you fear, and assure them they will get information as you learn it. Children want to be able to trust you.

- Encourage children to ask questions as often as they need to do so.

- Recognize crying or a tantrum for what it is — acting out rather than verbalizing fears and attempt to reassure the child. In reassuring him/her, let the child know that it is okay to feel sad, to cry and to get angry.

- When family or friends visit, include the child in the "how are you doing?" Remember your child may feel left out.

- Give an extra hug or "atta boy".

Chapter 6:
Things Kids Can Do That Help

Again, this was an easy question..."what would you tell other kids to do that might help them?" Here are their ideas; we hope they help others.

- Talk about your feelings!

- Tell people what's going on—ask for help and accept help that's offered.

- Don't be strong, it's ok to need help.

Time with your family members is valuable. — *Jillian, age 17*

- If you can, find other kids going through this, like in a support group

- Ask questions if you're confused

- Be aware of what helps you during bad times— we have a list that includes music journaling, art, physical activities like riding your bike, talking to a friend, being with pets

- Find ways to relax like meditation, deep breathing, yoga

- Be alone when you need to be alone

How Kids Alive Helped Us ...

- Makes cancer not feel so scary.

- Being around people who understand what you've been through

- It's fun and joyful

- In Kids Alive I love to have friends that can relate to what I am going through

- You talk about your feelings, it doesn't matter what you say.

- Break from cancer and the world

- Least judgmental place, it's a safe haven

- If a new kid joined, I would want them to know that it's a safe place to talk. This helped me because it let me talk about things that I wouldn't with my normal friends.

About Kids Alive

Kids Alive was founded in 1995 in response to the voiced concerns of participants in a breast cancer support group that there was a lack of organized support for the children of breast cancer patients. The next year Kids Alive expanded to include children whose parents had any cancer diagnosis. It has continued since 1995, meeting and supporting children ages 6-16. The purpose of Kids Alive is to serve children by helping them contend with the trauma of a parent's diagnosis of cancer by providing a secure and healthy environment in which they are free to express their feelings.

Kids Alive goals are to:

• To provide a safe, helpful environment for children of cancer patients to express their feelings.

• To create a place for a child to be a child... to experience fun, support and continuity of life... apart from catastrophic illness.

• To facilitate a better relationship between cancer patients and their families, reducing guilt and anxiety in children.

• To help parents interpret their children's behavior as adaptive to the trauma in the family and improve communication in the family.

• To develop awareness of resources for both parents and children.

For more information regarding Kids Alive, please visit www.kidsalivecolorado.org

Made in the USA
San Bernardino, CA
21 February 2015